UNLEASHING
the
Power of
FAITH

UNLEASHING
the
Power of
FAITH

David Yonggi Cho

Bridge-Logos

Orlando, Florida 32822

Bridge-Logos

Orlando, Florida 32822 USA

Unleashing the Power of Faith
Copyright © 2006 by Rev. David Yonggi Cho
First published in Korean, © 2001 by Seoul Logos Co.

Printed in the United States of America.

Library of Congress Catalog Card Number: 2005939117
International Standard Book Number 0-88270-095-2

Scripture quotations, unless otherwise stated, are from the *New International Version*. Copyright © 1973, 1978, 1984 by International Bible Society. Used by permission of Zondervan Publishing House.

G1.316.N.m606.35150

Contents

Part 1

The Functional Relationship Between Success and Language

Part 2

The Principle of Faith Energy

Part 3

Unleashing the Power of Faith

Foreword

The greatest threat posing a crisis for humanity today is the loss of hope. All over the world, there are regions marked by war, fear, and destruction. There are areas of extreme poverty and famine. Experts who diagnose modern times often ask, "Is there hope for humankind?" We can see what they mean by looking at society around us. Whether personally, socially, or on a national level, no matter how much hope one may start with, reality forces a person to lose that hope rather quickly.

At such times, how must Christians live in this world? Just as a baby has absolute trust in its mother, Christians must also live in absolute faith and trust in God. No matter how negative the world around us may be, we must not lose faith.

Faith itself is hope and has the power to make all things new.

When a man came to Christ with his son who was possessed by a legion of demons, asking what can be done, Christ stated, "'If you can'? Everything is possible for him who believes" (Mark 9:23). Having faith in Christ's words, when the man changed his mind and his words, his son's life changed completely.

A Christian must be of the mind and attitude that everything is possible through faith. Then you can live in control of your destiny and circumstances, a life of victory through faith. I pray that your life will be made anew through this book, so you can live in victory through faith and glorify God.

Dr. David Yonggi Cho
Senior Pastor
Yoido Full Gospel Church

Part 1

The Functional Relationship Between Success and Language

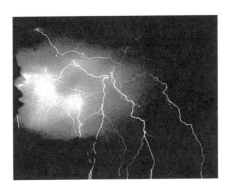

chapter 1

A New Mind and a New Language

According to the research of Dr. Constantin von Economo from Austria (1876-1931), the thickness of the brain, which is wrinkled like a walnut, is about 3 millimeters. However, when the brain is spread out, it is as large as a newspaper page. It also consists of around 14 billion nerve cells.

Even today, the brain remains one of the greatest mysteries. It is said that 90 percent of our knowledge about the brain has been discovered in the last 15 years, with still more questions. It is without doubt that the brain is indeed a true mystery.

According to another research by a brain specialist, the amount of the brain used by Goethe was 0.4 percent during his lifetime, by Einstein 0.6 percent, and there has not been a single person who has used more than 1 percent of his or her brain.

It is certain that God has given humankind an unlimited mental resource, but that we do not fully use what has been made available to us. If we were able to use all the potential we possess with the help of the Holy Spirit, a truly unimaginable world would be made available to us.

Americans and Europeans excel in various aspects. It is interesting to note that they live in countries influenced by Christianity. Culturally, they seek challenges and respond to them. They sailed around the world, discovered new land, and provided for the comforts of the modern world through their inventions, such as the automobile and airplanes.

Many of the schools, hospitals, orphanages, and convalescent centers in Korea are results of western

Christians who came and took on the challenge by faith. It is plain to see that the fundamental factor that improves the lives and circumstances of humankind, is based upon faith in God.

To live successful lives, we must have the firm belief, "it can be done," both in our physical and spiritual lives. Many people make the mistake of thinking that the hope they have is the same as faith.

"If only I could be wealthy … "

"If only I could succeed … "

"If only I could do great work for God … "

Such thoughts that entertain the word "if" are nothing more than wishes. They are not the thoughts of faith.

> *"I can do everything through him who gives me strength" (Philippians 4:13).*

"I can do." This is the declaration of faith.

When you think something is possible, you will be able to see the course of action to take. When you think something is impossible, you will find that it cannot be accomplished.

For humankind, there is a spiritual realm that transcends the physical and the mental realms.

> *"By faith we understand that the universe was formed at God's command, so that what is seen was not made out of what was visible" (Hebrews 11:3).*

When our spirits, which belong to the unseeable realm, confidently proclaim, "It can be done," we are filled with inspiration, revelation, and wisdom to find the way, even as the Holy Spirit aids us. However, when we proclaim, "It cannot be done," the spiritual realm is shut down automatically, and we cannot accomplish it.

1. Think Success

On a daily basis, I dream and pray about the evangelization of Korea and the whole world. I have always thought it to be possible. That is the reason for our Internet webcast ministry, which has been spreading the Gospel through the Internet all over the world. Also, in order to facilitate the evangelization of Korea, I have a dream of pioneering 500 churches in Korea over the next 10 years. Many have told me it would be impossible. However, the Holy Spirit has assured me, and I have been researching and putting the dream into action.

No matter what difficulties you may face, say to yourself, "I can succeed!" Continually think of succeeding. When you do so, you will indeed find success.

On the other hand, when you think, "Maybe I will fail," your very fear of failure will cause you to fail. I know of no person who thought of failure and succeeded.

There are instances where you will fail in spite of thinking of success. Many people have their faith shaken thinking, "I only thought of success; why did I fail?"

A deacon faced a day in court over a real estate matter. He prayed to God for help and only thought of winning the case. He stood before the judge with confidence. Unfortunately, the decision went against him. The devastated deacon said, "If God is alive, how could He do this to me?" His very faith was being put into question. Why did he lose his case in spite of diligent prayer and thinking of success?

When you study at a school, you pay tuition. From elementary to university, you need to pay a certain amount of tuition. No matter what it is you are learning, you need to pay a tuition fee for your education. It is the same in society. In any society, there is a price in learning the ways of survival in a society. When people invest hundreds of thousands of dollars in a business and fail in the business, they lament the loss of their hard-earned money. When people pay thousands of dollars to defend themselves in court but lose, they believe the money was a big waste. That is not so. It was tuition for a

greater learning experience, which could
even greater success.

Whether in society, at home, or at church, if we
are afraid to pay for the cost of learning from failure,
we may never find success. Although failure may
be a terribly bitter experience, it can be a learning
experience leading to success. Rather than
despairing over failure, you must be positive. You
must consider it as tuition toward success.

You should even accept your failure as part of
your future success. You should not think of
anything else except your future success. Think and
speak only of succeeding. Dream about success,
think success, and live a successful life. "Maybe I
will fail. What if I fail?" If you think like this and
despair, you will not have the productive energy to
accomplish what you desire. You must not be afraid
of failing, but think only of success. Of course that
success must be to glorify Christ.

2. Aim High

While I was a child, I heard many times from grown-ups, "When you draw something, start with a tiger in mind, and at least you will end up with a cat. If you start with a cat, the best you can do is a cat and maybe not even that."

They were telling me to aim high. The Bible says likewise.

"Open wide your mouth and I will fill it"
(Psalm 81:10).

As I have led my ministry for the last 46 years, I have always aimed high. Because I aimed so high, I prayed more than others, studied more than others, and made an effort much greater than others. I went about with great confidence. Actually, whether you aim high or not, making an effort to succeed is not much different. Isn't it better then to aim high?

3. Look at Success

In order to succeed, you must always picture yourself with a successful image. It is the principle of looking. Christians and non-Christians likewise, you must apply the principle of looking in order to succeed.

People who succeed even dress for success. It does not mean you need to wear expensive and flashy clothes. Like a successful person, you must dress cleanly and neatly. From the way you walk and the way you talk, your whole attitude must be that of a successful person. You must foster and develop your self-image.

> *"But you are a chosen people, a royal priesthood, a holy nation, a people belonging to God" (1 Peter 2:9).*

Rich people are those who always look upon themselves as being rich. Successful businessmen are those who always look upon themselves as being successful in business. Those who are respected by others are those who always think themselves respectable by others. Those who do not look at success, will not find success.

> *"What is seen was not made out of what was visible" (Hebrews 11:3).*

You must always look at the blueprint of success in your mind, which cannot be seen physically.

4. Pray Expecting Success

God is success itself. He has never failed. He is light itself. He has never been in darkness. He is health itself. He has never been ill. He is alive forever.

When we pray, which is to communicate with Him, we must "pray expecting success." Such a lamentation as, "I don't know what to do," is not a prayer expecting success. "Because You are with me, there will be a miracle." This is a prayer expecting success. The creator God can make all things possible. In order to move Him, we must pray with the right words.

In geometry, a line drawn between two points belongs to the first dimension. If thousands and thousands more lines are drawn, it becomes the second-dimensional plane. If two such planes meet, it becomes third dimensional. The first dimension is a part of the second dimension, which in turn is a part of the third dimension. This principle is around us in the real physical world. The world we live in is the three-dimensional realm. What governs this world? It is the fourth dimension, the spiritual world. The fourth-dimensional world can be better understood by Genesis 1:2:

> *"Now the earth was formless and empty,*
> *darkness was over the surface of the deep,*
> *and the Spirit of God was hovering over*
> *the waters."*

The original text of this verse describes the hovering of the Spirit of God, as a bird hovering over her eggs. In other words, the Spirit of God _er_ the waters, like a bird hovering

the "formless and empty" earth belongs to _the third_ dimension, the Holy Spirit belongs to the fourth dimension. With the Spirit of God hovering over the waters, God spoke to create the world. Then creation became a reality.

We must always pray to God in the spiritual fourth dimension.

"Oh God, take pity upon this ill man. Hover over him and heal him." When you pray for a sick person in this way, the Holy Spirit will indeed heal.

To pray is to ask for creative success. To pray is to hover over formless and empty reality in the fourth dimension ruled by the Holy Spirit, and to give light to reality.

You must succeed in your responsibilities, and continue to succeed in Christ. Only when you succeed can you be flush with joy and happiness. Those who succeed can perform a hard task without exhaustion. They work all night but are not tired.

When you succeed, you can be full of confidence, respected by others, have a comfortable life, and dream of a greater future.

In order to have a successful life, you must first think success. Aim high, and envision yourself as being successful. Pray expecting success. Success will indeed be yours.

chapter 2

The Power of the Mind
and Language

Once I had an opportunity to have breakfast with a very well known and respected neurosurgeon. He told me many things that have been discovered concerning the brain.

"Pastor, did you know that the speech center of the human brain dominates over all other nerves? According to the latest research, the speech center of the brain has very great influence over other nervous systems."

"I have been aware of that for quite some time."

"Really? How is it that you already knew this? This has only been recently published."

"I learned it from Dr. James."

"Dr. James?"

"Yes, he lived about two thousand years ago and was quite well known. He described the importance of the tongue and the language quite clearly. Now, let's look at James 3:1-12. Although the tongue is a small organ in our body, it can keep all of the body in check."

He was greatly surprised and began elaborating on his medical knowledge in this area. According to his knowledge, due to the greater influence of the speech center of the brain, it can control the body in the direction it so desires.

"When a person keeps saying, 'I am growing weaker,' the message is delivered to all the nerves of the body, and they say, 'Let's prepare to grow weaker. We must be weak under instructions from the brain.' Then the nerves actually begin to prepare to grow weaker.

"When a person says, 'I am unable and can't really accomplish this task,' all the nerves begin to reflect this message saying, 'That's right, the central nervous system instructs us that we would be incapable. We have to give up developing any ability. We must prepare to become incapable.' When a person keeps saying, 'I am too old and tired to do anything,' the speech center exercises its influence and controls the response of the body. All the nerves reflect the message and say, 'We are old. We are ready to be put into a grave. Let's prepare to decay.' If a person continues to say that he or she is old, the person will indeed grow older and die much more quickly."

He continued to explain:

"We must never lose our ambition and drive to live. When we lose the will to live, we will begin to say to ourselves that we no longer have a reason to live. Then all of our nerves will begin to shut down, and we will indeed die soon."

I mostly agreed with what the doctor was telling me. It reinforced my belief that positive confession through our lips becomes the foundation of success in our lives.

James 3:3 tells us that controlling our tongues will make it possible to control the whole body.

Your life is governed by what you say. If you continue to say that you are poor, you will indeed grow poorer. In the end, you will come to accept and be comforted by your very poverty. You may even want to be mired in that poverty.

However, if you repeat to yourself that you are able and will succeed, your physical body, soul, and spirit will be motivated by the message, and you will actually succeed.

Korean people have a habit of saying, "I'm dying. The heat is killing me. I'm so full I could die. I'm happy to death. It's so scary, I think I'll die."

Because of these negative words, maybe the Korean people have never known peace and have been involved in endless wars and conflicts throughout their 5,000-year history.

We must abandon this habit and always say positive things. Saying good and positive things should be our habit.

If you want to change, you must change your words. If you do not change the way you speak and the things you say, you cannot change fundamentally. If you desire your children to change, you must first teach them to speak positive words. If you desire irresponsible and rebellious youth to be well-adjusted grown-ups, you must first teach them a "new" language.

Where can we learn this "new" language? Through the Bible, we can learn the very best of languages. When in need, the Holy Spirit reminds us of the applicable verses in the Bible that will comfort us and make us soar and succeed.

Read the Bible on a daily basis, and meditate on it. Be governed by the language of the Bible. Use the language of faith. Fill your mind with words of productivity, progress, constructiveness, and victory. When you do so, you will live in great success.

chapter 3

Faith Energy

"Now faith is the substance of things hoped for, the evidence of things not seen."
(Hebrews 11:1, KJV)

1. Faith Is the Substance of Things Hoped For

Faith is the substance of what we hope for. The Greek word for substance is "hypostasis," which connotes "footing" and is also used for "a certificate of ownership."

We can say that faith is the footing of things hoped and wished for. We cannot set up anything on a fragile footing. Likewise, we can never lead lives of faith into success if our faith is weak.

Faith is also a certificate of title of things we hope for eagerly. What is a certificate of title? It's a collection of documents by which we can assert our ownership of land or a building. Therefore, when we hope and pray eagerly for something, and have certainty in our hearts as if we have a registered bond in our hands, that very security is faith.

Although you may not see any evidence of it with your eyes or hear any sound with your ears, even as your future seems dark, when faith energy starts to work within you and makes you think, "It's already come about," then you become a person of faith.

2. Faith Is the Evidence of Things Not Seen

Faith is the evidence of what we cannot see. When we have the substance of things hoped for in our hearts, we are certain as if they were already realized. That is faith. When we have such faith in us, Christ blesses us with the words; "It will be done just as you believed it would." To a person with such faith, there is nothing impossible.

There is actually nothing to be seen; however, when you pray, if you feel that things which are not as though they were, you are on the right track. Nothing is impossible at such point.

"'If you can'? said Jesus. "Everything is possible for him who believes'"
(Mark 9:23).

3. Faith Is the Energy of the Holy Spirit

Once we have that faith, we must declare our faith with our mouth and begin to use that faith. For example, when you begin to feel certain that you are being healed from your long illness through your prayers, you must begin to declare your faith; "I have been healed. I am well. Pain and suffering from deceit and lies, be gone from me!"

By what evidence and proof can you make such a declaration? It is by the promise of God:

> *"But he was pierced for our transgressions, he was crushed for our iniquities; the punishment that brought us peace was upon him, and by his wounds we are healed" (Isaiah 53:5).*

> *"Therefore I tell you, whatever you ask for in prayer, believe that you have received it, and it will be yours" (Mark 11:24).*

"Christ was wounded so that I may be healed. I should not be suffering. I am healthy." When you have faith through such a promise in the Bible, the Holy Spirit provides healing energy, so that you will indeed be well.

Though you are convinced that God will heal you, you may say, "Healed? No, I still hurt." However, if you do not declare your faith with your lips, your faith energy cannot work, and you will never experience a miracle.

It is the same way with the problems in your life. When you give your tithes and pray, you will feel the confidence of faith that God is indeed working to make your life rich and full of blessing. When you feel that faith, you must declare it with your mouth, and loose your faith energy to work in your life.

What does the Bible say?

"I tell you the truth, whatever you bind on earth will be bound in heaven, and

> *whatever you loose on earth will be loosed in Heaven" (Matthew 18:18).*

The Greek text of the Bible states the verse in the past tense. In other words, it is not something that will happen in the future, but has already happened.

"I am a blessed person."

"I am healthy."

"I am victorious in Christ."

Such positive confession paves the way for a shortcut to the blessing and the experience of God's miracles in your life.

4. *Faith Is the Unity of Belief and Words*

Today, many people fail in their faith because their words are different from their belief. When they come to church, they seem to have great faith that can move mountains. However, when they leave the church, they fall back to their negative thoughts and words, and all the productive energy that they had during the worship service ebbs away and vanishes.

Do you desire your faith to grow and your life to prosper continually? You must believe that you can bring about great changes in yourself, in your home, in your work place, and in your destiny. When you have such faith and assurance, it will indeed bring about great miracles in your life. Through your words and prayer, you must continue to declare such faith with your mouth. It will lead to a great change in your circumstances as well as your destiny. The Bible makes the following promise:

"The LORD will open the heavens, the storehouse of his bounty, to send rain on your land in season and to bless all the work of your hands. You will lend to many nations, but will borrow from none. The LORD will make you the head, not the tail, if you pay attention to the

> *commands of the LORD your God that I*
> *give you this day and carefully follow*
> *them, you will always be at the top, never*
> *at the bottom. Do not turn aside from any*
> *of the commands I give you today, to the*
> *right or to the left, following other gods*
> *and serving them"*
> *(Deuteronomy 28:12-14).*

Hold onto this promise of God. In your personal life, at home, and in your work place, you will indeed enjoy such blessing as mentioned in Deuteronomy 28.

When such faith energy continues to come forth through the declaration of your lips, you will be able to live a victorious life of faith.

5. *Faith Is Visible*

A hiker on a mountain slipped and fell down a cliff. Fortunately, as he was sliding down, he was able to grab hold of a small branch on a tree. He shouted out in terror,

"Is anyone there? Help me!"

Then he heard a voice saying, "I am here above you. I am your God."

"I am so glad You are here above me. God, help me please."

"Before I help you, I need to ask you one thing. Do you really believe in Me?"

"Of course, God. I go to church every Sunday and even perform volunteer service at the church. I believe in You."

"Good. Then let go of the branch you are holding onto."

"Um, pardon?"

"If you truly believe in Me, let go of that branch you are holding."

The man thought deeply for a long time, then he shouted, "Is there anyone else up there?"

Faith must be visible. Just because you can speak eloquently about faith, it does not mean you possess faith. Faith is the ability to grab onto that which cannot be seen. Faith is a volitional decision by the very actions you take.

Through deeds, your faith becomes visible. In the Bible, there are common elements in the miracles performed by Jesus Christ. Christ first saw the faith in people before He performed miracles.

It happened while Christ was at the home of Peter's mother-in-law. With the word of His coming, a big crowd had gathered at her home. The home and the yard outside the home were filled with people. Among the people, there was a man suffering from paralysis. Since he could not walk by himself, his friends brought him on a mat. However, with so many people gathered around, they simply could not bring him close to Christ. Certain that he would be healed if only they brought him to Christ, they decided to break through the ceiling of the home.

Bang! Bang! There came sounds of the ceiling being broken. Dust and debris must have begun to fall on Christ's head from the ceiling even as He was talking. People in the house must have become restless and curious. The men on the roof disregarded all protest coming from below and concentrated on breaking the roof because of their strong desire to meet Christ. Finally, a big hole opened up above Jesus Christ and a paralytic man on a mat was lowered down. When this was happening, the Bible states what Christ saw:

"Jesus saw their faith" (Luke 5:20).

The Bible states that Christ saw their faith. Seeing their faith, Christ commanded the paralytic man:

"I tell you, get up, take your mat and go home" (Luke 5:24).

As soon as Christ commanded the man, he did indeed get up and walk.

In Lystra, the apostle Paul also saw the faith of a person before performing a miracle. As Apostle Paul was preaching the gospel of Jesus Christ, there sat a man crippled since birth. Paul saw the man had faith to be healed and commanded him, "Stand up!" Instantly, the man stood up. A miracle!

In such ways, God sees the faith of a person before He allows the manifestation of miracles. It is written in James 2:17, "In the same way, faith by itself, if it is not accompanied by action, is dead."

God's miracles are based on visible faith.

Part 2

The Principle of
Faith Energy

chapter 4

Everything Depends on What You Think

An American tourist came to look at Niagara Falls. He went down to the foot of the falls and drank some water. Feeling refreshed from the water, he stood up to see a small sign that stood beside the water. Suddenly, he clutched his chest and contorted. With the help of those around him, he was taken to a hospital.

The sign that he saw had one word written on it, "POISON!" It was quite obvious why he was taken to a hospital.

As soon as the man saw a doctor at the hospital, he shouted, "I drank the water from Niagara Falls. There was a sign next to the water saying "POISON." Please, I need an antidote right away. I can feel the poison spreading throughout my body already."

When the doctor heard what the man said, he laughed out loud.

"Stop all the ruckus and get up, sir. The sign you saw did not say 'POISON.' The word used was actually the French word 'POISSON' with one more 's' than in the word 'POISON.' The French word 'POISSON' means 'fish.' Therefore, the sign was giving notice that the water was reserved for the protection of fish."

Your mind can have a devastating effect on your attitude. It is the same in your faith life. Depending on what you have in your mind, your faith life may change.

Recently, the changes sweeping throughout the world and in Korea as we face the 21st century require us to change our frame of mind. Rather than struggling with the changes, we must ride upon the waves of that change and head for the harbor of security and prosperity. To do so, our minds must be filled with positive and affirmative thinking.

We should not think, "I cannot do it. I am incapable. What can I do?"

Such negative thoughts only lead to a greater depression and despair. Those who give up will indeed only have failure to look forward to. Therefore, the thinking that "I cannot do" must be changed into "I can do."

You must stand strong. You must stand exactly where you are. And then, you must look toward hope.

If you practice the following five principles of spirituality, you will experience the greatest life.

chapter 5

The Principle of Rulership

*"Be fruitful and increase in number; fill
the earth and subdue it. Rule over the fish
of the sea and the birds of the air and over
every living creature that moves on the
ground" (Genesis 1:28).*

In Genesis 1, the reason is given why God
created humankind.

*"Let us make man in our image, in our
likeness, and let them rule over the fish of
the sea and the birds of the air, over the
livestock over all the earth, and over all*

the creatures that move along the ground"
(Genesis 1:26).

Humankind was created in the image and likeness of God and received the right to rule over all things on this earth. Knowing this, Satan used every possible means to make humankind fall from grace and forfeit such authority.

Through Satan's scheme, humankind did indeed fall from grace, lost the image of God, and a seed of evil was planted in the ability to rule over all things. Look upon nature and the earth which humankind has conquered. People have trampled upon the earth, polluted it and destroyed it. Wherever humankind conquers and rules, the seeds of evil are planted.

To those who accept Christ as Savior, there is the greatest blessing of recovering that lost image of God.

As such, you and I, having accepted Christ as Savior, have been crucified with Christ on the cross, and have become a new creation.

To those who are created anew in the image of God, He gives the right of rulership once again. Therefore, to Christians, there cannot be any failure or state of being trampled underfoot. There is only victory for Christians.

> *"Therefore, if anyone is in Christ, he is a new creation; the old has gone, the new has come!" (2 Corinthians 5:17).*

We are no longer slaves to our destinies, slaves to our environment, and slaves to our circumstances; we are the rulers of everything on the earth.

Although God has given this authority, it is heartbreaking to see some Christians who are unable to exercise this authority and fail to live blessed lives.

How can we rule over our environment?

1. Retain the Image of a Ruler in Your Heart

In order to live as a ruler, you must have an image of yourself as a ruler. If you are filled with an inferiority complex, a negative mindset, disappointment, failure, and poverty, God cannot help you.

Once you have been forgiven of your sins through Jesus Christ, you must think, "I have been created anew in the image of God in Christ. I have been blessed to rule over everything. Therefore, I will enjoy good health and all will go well with me, even as my soul is getting along well. I will also have life to the full." When you have such assurance, it will be as you believe.

As such, you must first have an image of yourself as a ruler in your heart.

When hardship and trouble come upon me, I always meditate upon this passage in the Bible:

> *"The LORD sits enthroned over the flood; the LORD is enthroned as King forever" (Psalm 29:10).*

With this passage in mind, I envision myself as a ruler.

"Like the Lord enthroned over the flood, I will ride upon all circumstances and troubles as I ride to victory."

When you repeat these words to yourself and thank God, all fear will dissipate and the assurance in your heart will become even greater.

Such grace has not been given to me only, but to all Christians.

You should learn to shout, "I am a ruler over my environment and circumstances."

We have lived like the wind blowing and the water flowing, resenting our ill-fated lives, and we have been slaves of destiny. But now we can conquer the demons, sin, illness, and poverty because we have been born again as rulers.

Our rebirth is not to become slaves to despair once again. Our rebirth is to make us into rulers over the environment. You should have the attitude; "I am a ruler." You must have this image of yourself in your heart.

2. *Have God at the Center of Your Life*

For us to exercise such authority to rule, we must have God at the center of our lives.

Having the right to rule in this world means having the right to vicarious execution of God's authority. As such, if our lives are not connected to God, we cannot exercise the right to rule over this world. That's why God tests us to see if we indeed have Him in the center of our lives before He gives the right to us.

When Moses led the Israelites and came to Kadesh Barnea, he sent twelve scouts to explore Canaan. Why? Did God command Moses to send them because He did not know the situation in Canaan? No. Before giving the Israelites the right to rule over Canaan, God wanted to know what lay at the center of their hearts.

The twelve scouts explored the land for forty days and returned to give their report. Ten among the twelve gave a negative report.

> *"And they spread among the Israelites a bad report about the land they had explored. They said, 'The land we explored devours those living in it. All the people we saw there are of great size. We saw the Nephilim there (the descendants of Anak come from the Nephilim). We seemed like grasshoppers in our own eyes, and we looked the same to them'"*
> *(Numbers 13:32, 33).*

Hearing this report, that night all the Israelites raised their voices and wept aloud. They cried out for the return to Egypt. However, Joshua and Caleb gave a completely different report.

> *"Only do not rebel against the LORD.*
> *And do not be afraid of the people of the*
> *land, because we will swallow them up.*
> *Their protection is gone, but the LORD is*
> *with us. Do not be afraid of them"*
> *(Numbers 14:9).*

The ten scouts did not have God in the center of their hearts, but rather allowed their humanistic ways to take the center, so that they felt only desperation at seeing the land of Canaan. On the other hand, as Joshua and Caleb centered their lives on God, they could be convinced of the hope and possibility of seeing anything in any situation.

As a result, the ten scouts who gave a negative report and the people who listened to their report and grumbled against God, all died without entering Canaan. Only Joshua and Caleb were allowed to enter Canaan and receive their inheritance. To Joshua and Caleb, who focused only on God and thought positively with faith, He gave the right to rule over Canaan.

In such a way, before we are given the right to rule over our circumstances and the world, God tests us. Just as we must pass certain tests in order to enter a higher level of an educational institution like high school, college, or university, we are tested whenever we face a higher level of circumstance given by God. We cannot take a step back and avoid this test. Until we successfully pass the test, we will face hardships.

"No one who puts his hand to the plow and looks back is fit for service in the kingdom of God" (Luke 9:62).

We must all face the test given us by God with positive attitudes and grasp the limitless possibility. When we do so, we can pass the test to conquer and rule over our circumstances and to live powerful lives.

chapter 6

The Principle of Looking

"So Moses made a bronze snake and put it up on a pole. Then, when anyone was bitten by a snake and looked at the bronze snake, he lived" (Numbers 21:9).

The principle of looking plays an important role when it comes to being blessed by God. Let us read the words Christ spoke to Nicodemus:

"Just as Moses lifted up the snake in the desert, so the Son of Man must be lifted up, that everyone who believes in him may have eternal life" (John:14, 15).

There is a very important lesson to be learned from this passage. Christ came to redeem humankind from sin. In the passage, it states that Christ must also "be lifted up," which presumes humankind has been already spiritually bitten by a venomous snake. Spiritually, humankind has been robbed, beaten, and left to die by the forces of evil since having grumbled, complained, and disobeyed God.

The world around us is filled with darkness and despair. All of us who are oppressed by Satan due to our sin cannot help but be condemned to death. However, Christ said that He had to be lifted up. It meant that He would take upon Himself the full force of Satan's power as He went up on the Cross. Anyone who looks at Christ on the cross will be moved from darkness to light and from death to life. This is the principle of looking.

We can see also that God taught Abraham this very principle of looking to bless him. As Abraham reached an age at which he could only despair of not having any children, God appeared to him and commanded him to look up at the heavens and count the stars (Genesis 15:5). From that time on, Abraham began to look at the stars as his own descendants through his eyes of faith. As such, he did indeed become an ancestor of countless numbers of offspring.

There are also cases of failure when looking upon the wrong thing. One in particular was concerning Lot's wife. As Sodom and Gomorrah fell toward destruction, God commanded Lot's family to look forward and never back. Even so, Lot's wife looked back and became a pillar of salt (Genesis 19:26). Her sin was looking back. As she watched Sodom and Gomorrah fall, she also brought about her own destruction.

Eve, in the Garden of Eden, was a similar case. It resulted from the principle of looking that she ate from the tree of the knowledge of good and evil. She saw that the fruit of the tree was good for food and pleasing to the eye and also desirable. She was drawn to the fruit and ate of it (Genesis 3:6).

David also committed great sin resulting from looking at the wrong thing. As the army of Israel was out fighting the Ammonites, David remained and was resting comfortably in Jerusalem. Then one evening, he walked around on the roof of the palace and saw a woman taking a bath. He was infatuated with her and committed adultery. The sin of adultery led to another sin of murder. When the woman became pregnant, he had her husband sent to the front line where the fighting was the fiercest, in order to have him killed (2 Samuel 11:2-15).

What you look at is very important.

We live in this world, which is much like a desert. As we pass through this desert, at times we fall upon and are bitten by a venomous snake, which is by Satan. When we have suffered such a bite, what must we do?

We must look at Jesus Christ. Just as those dying from venomous snake bites had to look at the bronze snake on a pole, when we look at Jesus Christ on the cross, we receive life to the full, and we experience the great miracle of having our spirit, mind, and body restored.

1. Look at the Forgiveness of Your Sins

Although there may be a difference in degree, there are none without sin. Just as you inherit your genes from your parents, every person is born in sin because everyone inherits the sin of Adam. This sin only deepens as each person commits more sin after birth.

What can be done to solve the problem of sin? It cannot be dealt with through any religious ceremony. It cannot be answered through any amount of money. The only way to rid oneself of sin is to look at Jesus Christ who died on the cross. When you look at Jesus Christ on the cross, you will be filled with the joy and assurance of having your sins forgiven.

"Without the shedding of blood there is no forgiveness" (Hebrews 9:22).

2. Look at the Fullness of the Holy Spirit

When you look at Christ crucified and bleeding on the cross, you can experience the anointing of the Holy Spirit.

When you pray looking at the suffering Christ, the Holy Spirit comes into you and helps you to pray in tongues, which is a marvelous spiritual experience.

Look at the Cross. Look at Jesus Christ. When you do so, the fullness of the Holy Spirit will come upon you as it does to all that are forgiven.

When you are filled with the Holy Spirit, your heart and mind become fertile. If your barren heart and mind become fertile, whatever you plant through prayer will result in a harvest 30, 60, and 100 times greater.

Look at the Cross and take the water of the Holy Spirit that Jesus pours on you. The fullness of the Holy Spirit will fill you, your family, and your environment. All problems and troubles will drown in the water of the Holy Spirit.

3. Look at Divine Healing

Prior to being nailed upon the cross, Christ was given 39 lashes according to the laws and customs of that time. His flesh must have been torn very badly. He must have also bled profusely. Why did He have to suffer in such a way? The Bible tells us the reason for such suffering:

"By his wounds you have been healed"
(1 Peter 2:24).

In order to provide us with health, He endured such severe suffering. Whether it is mental illness, physical illness or spiritual illness we are facing, we must look at the injured body of Christ. When we do so, we will be made well from illness.

4. Look at Wealth

In order to redeem us from circumstantial and environmental hardship, Christ was hung on the cross. Christ lived in poverty all of His life. His life started poorly, being born in a manger. Until the day He died on the cross, He lived a poor life, and He had no place to lay His head.

Why did the Son of God live in such poverty? The Bible tells us the reason:

> *"For you know the grace of our LORD Jesus Christ, that though he was rich, yet for your sakes he became poor, so that you through his poverty might become rich"*
> *(2 Corinthians 8:9).*

If poor parents worked and saved money for their children but the children would not spend the money because they thought they should follow the example of their parents and live in poverty, this would not be the will of their parents.

> *"Christ redeemed us from the curse of the Caw by becoming a curse for us, for it is written: 'Cursed is everyone who is hung on a tree.' He redeemed us in order that the blessing given to Abraham might come to the Gentiles through Christ Jesus, so that by faith we might receive the promise of the Spirit" (Galatians 3:13, 14).*

It is a basic and fundamental grace coming from faith in Jesus that we enjoy good health and that all may go well with us, even as our soul is getting along well.

5. Look at the Hope of Heaven

Every person is like a pilgrim. There is not a single person who can remain forever on this earth. The Bible tells us:

> *"Why, you do not even know what will
> happen tomorrow. What is your life? You
> are a mist that appears for a little while
> and then vanishes" (James 4:14).*

We must all leave our bodies behind. After death, some receive eternal life while others receive eternal punishment. Those who accept Christ as Savior receive eternal life; however, those who don't accept Him receive eternal punishment. When Christ comes again, those who believe in Him receive eternal life to be resurrected in glory and to reside with Him forever.

For Christ to heal our spirits and bodies and to bless us is like letting us taste life in Heaven. That is why we do not need to despair over the storms we may face as we pass through the hardship-filled desert of life. We must live with the hope of eternal Heaven. The life looking toward heaven drives away despair and disappointment and attracts joy and gratitude.

chapter 7

The Principle of Sowing and Reaping

"Still other seed fell on good soil, where it produced a crop—a hundred, sixty or thirty times what was sown"
(Matthew 13:8).

No matter how dry a desert may be, if a river begins to run through it, it becomes fertile, and living creatures start to revive in it. Because of this, every ancient civilization grew near a river.

The Chinese civilization grew around the Yellow River, and the Indian civilization grew around the Indus and the Ganges. The civilization of Mesopotamia grew around the Tigris and the Euphrates Rivers, while that of Egypt around the Nile River.

In the hearts and souls of all who have accepted Christ as their Savior, the living water of God flows through them.

> *"Whoever believes in me, as the Scripture has said, streams of living water will flow from within him" (John 7:38).*

> *"He is like a tree planted by streams of water, which yields its fruit in season and whose leaf does not wither. Whatever he does prospers" (Psalm 1:3).*

Everyone who has accepted God has the river of life flowing through him or her and can taste the abundant grace of God.

Although the land is fertile from the river, if seeds are not planted, you cannot reap from the land. Without planting the seed of faith, we cannot experience the power of God.

There was a major fire in Chicago. When reporters from every major newspaper arrived, the buildings were on fire. In the midst of the burnt buildings was the church building of Pastor Moody, also burnt to the ground. A reporter went to Pastor Moody and said, "You've always preached that because God is alive and Almighty, He could make anything possible if you ask Him. Why did God let His church burn down?"

Pastor Moody answered him, "I've always been praying to God to give me a big church. This is God's answer. In order to build a big church, I would have had to spend a lot of money just to tear down the old building. He has just saved me great expense."

The reporter was flabbergasted. Pastor Moody was residing in the old church and barely escaped with only the pajamas he was wearing. The reporter asked him again, "Do you have the money to build a new church?"

Pastor Moody showed him the worn Bible he was holding under his arm and said, "I wasn't able to bring out any checks or money from the church. However, I've brought out the limitless source of God's fund. Soon you will see a big and great church being built right on this spot."

After the fire, Pastor Moody went to England to have revival meetings, and England had a great revival. When he was returning to America, something completely unexpected happened. Many of the people who were blessed by Pastor Moody's sermons during the revival meetings collected a large sum of money for the new church to be built. With the money, Pastor Moody was able to build a greater church on the very spot where the old one had burned.

You must remember, even though the heavens may seem to crash down upon you and the earth may seem to collapse around you, not even one letter in the Word of God will ever change.

*"Heaven and earth will pass away, but
my words will never pass away"
(Matthew 24:35).*

People you know will pass away, fashions come
and go, and even theology or a denomination may
not last forever. However, the Word of God will
never pass away. In the Word of God, the Bible,
there are around 32,500 promises. These promises
are not given selectively, more to some, less to
others. The promises are given to every Christian
equally.

When I visited Europe, some said, "You have
been especially anointed by God, and that is the
reason for so many miracles from God through
you."

That is absolutely not true. The 66 books in the
Bible are not given to me only. They are given to all
people equally. However, only those who do not
doubt the Bible, but place their faith wholly upon
it, can experience the miracles of God. Many people
believe the Word of God, but they fail to fully

practice their faith. This is why they do not experience the miracles of God.

It is the problem of your heart. Depending on what kind of heart, the seed of the Word of God results in different fruit.

In Matthew 13, Christ tells a parable of a man sowing seeds. He describes hearts like the path, rocky places, thorns, and good soil. From the first three kinds of heart, there cannot be any harvest. Only the heart like good soil can produce a crop—a hundred, sixty or thirty times. Should those who have hearts like the first three mentioned give up all together? No. No matter what kind of heart you may have, you can change it to a heart like good soil.

1. The Seed Along the Path

"Then he told them many things in parables, saying. 'A farmer went out to sow his seed. As he was scattering the seed, some fell along the path, and the birds came and ate it up'" (Matthew 13:3, 4).

If a seed falls onto good soil, it is covered with soil, so that birds cannot come to eat it. However, if it falls upon a path, it is quite visible and birds will find it easily.

It describes those who hear the Word of God and understand it, but fail to take care of the seed of the Word, since they are busy with the things of this world. They come to church each Sunday, but their minds are always filled with their work, their businesses, their country club and so on. Such people cannot produce anything.

Such hearts can become good soil if they are dug deeply, plowed and overturned. Just as there isn't any inherently good soil, no one inherently has a good heart. A path becomes fertile and good by turning it over. Then, how can we plow and overturn our hearts like a path?

1) We Must Plant the Seed of the Word

Planting the seed of the Word of God means to realize and understand the Word of God in our hearts. No matter how many sermons you hear and Bible studies you attend, if you don't understand the meaning of the Word of God, it is useless. You must understand the Word of God.

It happened while I was leading a service in a country church. No matter how earnestly I delivered the message, the congregation was lukewarm. I was feeling so frustrated. I looked at an old woman and asked her this question; "Do you believe in Christ?"

"Of course, I do," she answered. She spoke rather confidently.

"Do you believe you will go to Heaven after death?" I asked her again.

"Well, I will find out when I die, won't I?"

How is it possible for people to go to Heaven if they say they believe in Christ, yet they are not certain of Heaven and eternal life? There are people who have been coming to church for a long time, yet have not planted the seed of salvation in their hearts.

"Yet to all who received him, to those who believed in his name, he gave the right to become children of God" (John 1:12).

Rather than just knowing verses about salvation like the above, when you understand them deeply in your heart and are convicted by them, the seed of salvation is planted in you.

If you sow, it is the law of nature that you will reap. Once we plant the seed of salvation, we must believe that it will yield the fruit of salvation; if you plant the seed of prayer for healing, you must envision the fruit of divine healing.

For us to plant the seed of the Word, we must meditate upon the Word of God and live worshiping God, whether we are in church or at home. We must also study the Bible. As we do so, we begin to understand the Bible, and the seed of the Word will be planted in us. Finally we can reap its fruits.

2) We Must Obey

Once we comprehend the truth of the Word of God, we must obey. After having understood the truth of the Word of God, if you do not obey, you will not have faith.

> *"As the body without the spirit is dead, so faith without deeds is dead"* (James 2:26).

If you suffer from an illness, you should meditate deeply upon the verse, "By his wounds you have been healed" (1 Peter 2:24). Christ was wounded and bled, so that He could heal us; you must accept this truth in spirit. Then you must act and think as if you have already been healed. That is obedience. When you do so, God will indeed shine down upon you the light of divine healing.

Many people make the mistake of thinking, "When God blesses me, I will obey."

Others think, "If God heals me first, I will obey." It is like hitching a horse behind a wagon and expecting to go somewhere.

Faith follows obedience. It is written in 1 Samuel 15:22, "To obey is better than sacrifice, and to heed is better than the fat of rams." When the Holy Spirit opens your mind and makes you understand the truth of the Word of God, you must quickly obey. Through your obedience you must let the seed of the Word of God grow.

3) We Must Wait with Faith

Faith is based on the Word of God, rather than on the senses. Although you may not see any evidence with your eyes, nor hear with your ears, nor touch anything with your hands, you must stand firm upon the Word of God. Ignoring the Word of God and saying, "I believe," are quite useless.

Peter was able to walk on the water even as the waves crashed around him because he placed his trust in Christ's words and only looked at Him. However, when he turned from His words and looked at the waves rising around him, he began to sink into the water.

Once you understand and obey the Word of God, you must believe without doubt that it will be accomplished. You must not doubt and think, "Will God truly keep His promise?"

When I was a child, I planted a small yam plant in the corner of the yard of my home and watered it every day. However, I was so curious about how much it was growing, that I dug it up every two or three days. Not long afterward, the plant dried up and died. In order to harvest some yams, I should have waited until fall. But I couldn't be patient. By digging up the plant so soon, I did not give it enough time to take root in the ground.

Our faith is much the same. Once we understand the truth of the Word of God, we must obey. Then we must be patient until the miracle of God is manifested. Whether in good times or bad, we must wait patiently.

In farming, it is not good to have sunshine everyday. An ample amount of rain and sunshine is necessary. At times, wind also helps a harvest to grow.

In the same way, we will not always enjoy bright days in our faith lives. At times our businesses may falter, our families may face difficulties, or we may suffer illnesses. There are many troubles and trials we may face. However, we must not let such adverse circumstances sway our hearts and turn us away from the Word of God.

If you have made the decision to believe and obey the Word of God, you must stand firm upon it and wait. When you do so, you will experience the miracle of God.

4) We Must Declare Continuously

After a farmer plants the seed, he must continuously tend the growing crop; that is, he must weed and also cover the root with soil so that it isn't exposed on the ground. Even in our lives of faith, there is the necessity of covering the root with soil through our declaration of faith.

Modeling after God who calls things that are not as if they were, we must declare things that are not yet as if they already were.

"I have been saved."

"I have been blessed."

"I have been healed."

"My business is running well."

You should not declare such faith statements only when thing are going well. You should also declare them when things are not going so well. Even though you are in distress and trouble, you must declare with faith that God will indeed work in your life. When you do so, God is delighted with your faith and allows you to experience His miracles.

2. *The Seed on Rocky Places*

After God sows the seed of the Word, He tests us to see if we can truly bear fruit. Those who have no root will quickly abandon the Word they have believed and turn to the world when in times of trouble and hardship. Christ likened such people to rocky places.

Rocky places are full of rocks and stones under a thin layer of soil covering the surface. Seeds, which fall upon such places, spring up quickly, but because they have no root, they are scorched and wither soon.

By removing the stones and rocks and leveling the ground, rocky places can turn into good soil. In much the same way, no matter how full of rocks and stones someone's heart may be, the love of God can remove them and turn his or her heart into good soil.

3. The Seed Among Thorns

Some seeds fell among thorns. The seeds took root and began to grow. However, the plants were choked by the thorns and could not grow anymore.

When I led a crusade in Germany, a drunk man approached me and said, "Pray and heal me!" I said to him, "I am not a magician who heals people. I am a witness for Christ." I did not pray for the man. He did not seem to believe in God, only wanted to be rid of his illness. Such desire without faith is nothing more than greed. In such hearts, the Word of God cannot bear anything.

The one who has a heart of thorns is a person who hears the Word but cannot bear any fruit because of worldly greed.

Seeds that fall among thorns cannot reach full growth and will wither soon. However, even such ground can be made into good soil and bear abundant fruit by removing all thorns and overturning the soil.

All of us have different kinds of hearts. Regardless of what state our hearts are in, they can be made into hearts of good soil. Hearts full of thorns and weeds can be cleared by the sword of the Word, and cold hearts can be warmed by the fire of the Holy Spirit. Although you do not have a heart of good soil, you don't need to be discouraged.

In your hearts, continuously plant the seed of the Word of God from Genesis to Revelation. Then, tend the seed of the Word by putting it in practice. When you do so, your life will bear the fruit of the blessing of God in abundance.

chapter 8

The Principle of Giving and Receiving

"Give, and it will be given to you. A good measure, pressed down, shaken together and running over, will be poured into your lap. For with the measure you use, it will be measured to you" (Luke 6:38).

Many Christians say they believe in God, yet they look downtrodden, worn-out and lifeless. It is because they lack the vitality of faith. One of the causes of such lack in faith vitality is their lack of knowledge concerning the principle of giving and receiving. Those who delight to give to others are always full of grace and the Holy Spirit. The more you give to others, the more joy the Holy Spirit will give to you. You will also enjoy blessing from God that surpasses what you give to others.

In such a way, the key to being blessed by God is to first give to others. When you are led by the Holy Spirit to give to others, it opens your heart and through that opened heart, God blesses you.

Take the example of the Sea of Galilee and the Dead Sea. The Sea of Galilee continues to release water into the Dead Sea. The water in the Sea of Galilee is always fresh and clean. Meanwhile, the Dead Sea turns into water that cannot retain life. Nothing can live in the Dead Sea because it continues only to receive water, but doesn't release water. So it became the water of death. New blessing will flow upon you only when you give.

Around every one of us, there are those who are searching for our helping hands. We must learn to express our love to them. If you do not open your hands to others, you cannot expect God to bless you.

God works through the principle of giving and receiving. When we give first, God blesses us 30, 60, 100 times.

The famous steel tycoon, Andrew Carnegie, once said, "The reason I am running this factory and business is so that each person who works here can have a bank account and a dream."

His business vision was not to become wealthy alone, but also for others. He wanted to share more of his wealth with those who worked for him. He helped them plan for the future and live in hope. As a result, those who worked for him were encouraged and worked even harder, which turned his business into a world-class business.

Many pastors from around the world ask me for the secret of church growth. They ask, "How can I make my church grow?" I always answer them, "Help the people who come to your church to succeed and be blessed by God. They will in turn bless you and bring success to you as well."

Having a blessed and peaceful family is the same. First give your love and concern to your family. Problems begin when you only expect to receive instead of giving.

It may be a worldly principle to seek only your benefit without giving to others, but the principle of heaven is to give to others first, no matter how much you have. When we first give to others, God gives to us by a good measure, shaken together and running over.

chapter 9

The Principle of
Priority in Seeking

*"But seek first his kingdom and his
righteousness, and all these things will be
given to you as well" (Matthew 6:33).*

T hose who believe in and serve God must first
    prioritize. Christians must first love God, then
love their neighbors as themselves.

Many Christians understand the importance of
loving God, but they do not practice love for their
neighbors. Also, there are many cases of Christians

who have selfish love for themselves and cause their neighbors to suffer because of it. Look at those who love themselves selfishly. They are conceited, arrogant, loveless and irreconcilable. It is quite obvious that they cause suffering to those around them.

Only considering the relationship between oneself and God as being important while neglecting to care for one's neighbors is wrong. Practicing selfish love for oneself is also not righteous in God's eyes. A righteous life in God is to have a vertical relationship of love with Him while maintaining a balanced horizontal love with one's neighbors.

For us to live happy and righteous lives, we must have a balance of love for God and our neighbors. It is important that we prioritize what we must do first. According to the order of priority, we must pray, seek, and practice doing them. Those who fail to understand what they need to do first and last can only live unhappy lives. For Christians, what must we do first above all else? Christ said,

"But seek first his kingdom and his righteousness, and all these things will be given to you as well" (Matthew 6:33). The verse clearly tells us what we must do first.

1. Seek First His Kingdom

We must first seek "His kingdom." Seeking His kingdom means seeking the spiritual Heaven that is manifested through the Cross of Jesus Christ. His kingdom is where those who have been forgiven through the Cross reside.

Those who have become citizens of Heaven through faith in Jesus Christ must not focus their goals on this corruptible world. Christians have the kingdom of Heaven as their final destination and walk through this life in faith.

This world was full of sin, unrighteousness, the curse, illness, poverty, despair and death because of the fall of Adam. But since Christ came to this world, the good news of Heaven has been spread, and the miracles of Heaven have been taking place in this world.

The picture of Heaven Christ revealed to us, is one of forgiveness of sin and fullness of the Holy Spirit. It is one of being freed from the curse and being filled with the blessing of Abraham. Being healed and enjoying good health and wealth, where all of us will be filled with eternal life is Heaven.

We must not only experience this Heaven, but also share it with our neighbors.

2. Seek His Righteousness

Christians must first seek the kingdom of Heaven and also do their best to accomplish His righteousness on this earth.

Above all else, Christians must practice righteousness in their lives. God is with the righteous.

Christians must seek social righteousness. Christ came to this world to become an eternal friend to sinners, the poor, and the sick. Christ brought the righteousness of God into society. Christians who are followers of Christ must be an example of Him and make an effort to establish social righteousness.

Where righteousness is trampled underfoot, there is only formality and hypocrisy. Christians must pray and strive in order to establish righteousness in their personal lives, society, and nation. Between God and Christians, there is a vertical relationship while a horizontal relationship exists between Christians and their neighbors, society, and nation. Should Christians be satisfied with merely coming to church for worship and fellowship while ignoring the corruption and suffering in their society and nation, the Church and Christians are failing in their mission.

Christ states that when Christians seek His kingdom and His righteousness first, "all these things" would be given to them as well. When the righteousness of God is established in the economic and political realm of a society, the problems of "what to eat and drink" can be solved, and the corruption of the politicians and crime will disappear. A society full of sin and injustice will have a new order of harmony.

Rather than seeking that which we need, we must first seek the kingdom of God and His righteousness. When we do so, our material needs are met. However, when we lay aside God's kingdom and His righteousness and seek only our needs, that is wrong faith.

No matter how much effort a farmer may make to grow plants, if there is no rain or sunshine, his work comes to nothing. In the same way, no matter how much Christians may pray and seek blessing from God, if God does not bless them, it is useless. God will bless you, only when you seek first His kingdom and His righteousness.

chapter 10

The Principle of the Crowd

The principle of the crowd can be understood by the saying, "Birds of a feather flock together." Swallows flock together with other swallows, as ducks flock together with other ducks. This principle can be applied to the spiritual realm. Those who are always complaining flock with others who always complain. Those who are creative and productive flock with others who are the same.

In Mark 5:22-43, there is a rather dramatic scene of Christ bringing a girl back to life who had died.

One day as a large crowd gathered around Christ by the lake, Jairus, the synagogue ruler, approached Christ and asked Him to heal his daughter who was very sick. As Christ was accompanying Jairus to his home, some servants came running and said that his daughter had died, and there would be no need for Christ to come. However, Christ gave Jairus hope that He could still help her, and He continued going to his home.

When they arrived, there was already a commotion, with people crying and wailing for the dead girl. Christ went in and said to them, "Why all this commotion and wailing? The child is not dead but asleep" (Mark 5:39). But they laughed at Him. Christ sent them all out and took Peter, James and John who were of great faith, and the child's father and mother into the room where the girl was. He then performed a miracle and brought her back to life.

Christ used the principle of the crowd in order to bring the girl back to life. He only took those who had faith, and He performed the miracle.

We are affected by whom we associate. If we associate and have fellowship with those who have faith, we will have faith. If we associate with those who have positive minds, we will also have positive minds. In the same way, the principle of the crowd also results in God's blessing. If you desire to be blessed with things of Heaven, you should associate and have fellowship with those who have experience of such blessing.

The power of Christ is the same yesterday, today, and forever. However, such power of Christ is not manifested in a crowd of unbelievers, but only in a crowd of believers.

Christ did not do many miracles in His hometown, Nazareth. The Bible states the reason:

"And he did not do many miracles there because of their lack of faith"
(Matthew 13:58).

God does not manifest His miracle in a crowd of unbelievers. Look around you. Are there crowds of people who are negative and complain about their lives? Among a crowd of such people, the miracles of God will not be manifested. However, if you are among those who have firm faith, you will experience great miracles of God.

The blessing of God enters into us when our hearts are filled with positive and productive faith. Therefore, for us to be blessed, we must first fill our hearts and minds with positive and productive faith by associating with those who are filled with such faith.

So far, we have studied the spiritual principles of blessing according to the Bible. How much we are blessed by God in our lives of faith depends on how much we obey the spiritual principles of blessing.

Part 3

Unleashing the
Power of Faith

chapter 11

Seven Steps to a Productive Life

Nowhere in the Bible can a passage be found that says Christians must live in material need or in failed and depressed lives. The Bible promises all that you need.

"And God is able to make all grace abound to you, so that in all things at all times, having all that you need, you will abound in every good work"
(2 Corinthians 9:8).

In the Bible, those who were blessed by God not only lived in spiritual well being, but also in material wealth.

Take the example of Job. He was the richest man in the East. Although he was tested and lost everything he had ever owned, after the test he was blessed twice as much as he had before (Job 42:10).

In the case of Isaac, he obeyed God's command and as a result, he planted crops and reaped a hundredfold. He became rich, and his wealth continued to grow until he became very wealthy (Genesis 26:12, 13).

Jacob went to his uncle's home empty handed, but when he returned to his hometown, he became a great rich man (Genesis 31:17, 18).

Joseph was sold into Egypt as a slave, but he became ruler of all Egypt and helped feed many nations (Genesis 41:41).

Apostle Paul went to many places to witness for Christ. In the Bible it does not say that Paul was a burden to anyone (1 Thessalonians 2:9;

2 Thessalonians 3:8). He supported himself while he preached the Gospel.

In the Bible, we can easily find that those who served God were wealthy. That is because the Lord of the earth, sea and Heaven is our Father, our God.

God does not ignore His children and let them worry about what to eat and what to wear. Such worries are for non-Christians. Such basic needs are met by God when Christians seek first the kingdom of God and His righteousness.

Since God even feeds and clothes non-Christians, would He abandon His children whom He purchased with His own blood? For His glory and name, He blesses us.

The problem is our attitude toward faith. We must have the right attitude of faith to receive and enjoy the blessings that God has prepared for us.

In this book, there are seven steps to a productive life, which lead to the blessings of God. The seven principles are in concordance with the steps that God used to create the world.

If you understand and use these principles, you will indeed experience the amazing miracles of God in your life.

Through the seven steps, darkness can turn to light, disorder to order, death to life, and ugliness to beauty. In place of poverty will come wealth, and you will experience the wondrous miracle of your sadness turning into joy.

Now let us explore the secret within.

chapter 12

Wait for the Guiding Light

*"In the beginning God created the
heavens and the earth. Now the earth was
formless and empty, darkness was over the
surface of the deep, and the Spirit of God
was hovering over the waters. And God
said, 'Let there be light,' and there was
light" (Genesis 1:1-3).*

To bring order to chaos, first God created light.
In our lives, which are filled with formless and
empty darkness, we must first call out for light

saying, "Let there be light." Just as light shows the path even in the darkest of night, when light shines down on our lives, we are able to see the path we must take in our lives. How can we let such light shine in our lives?

We must pray sincerely to God, "Let light shine upon us!" When we have the assurance that He shines the light upon us, we must declare this with our lips. When we do so, light will be given to us in the form of dreams and ideas.

A sister in our church had a husband who had mistakenly co-signed for a friend to make a huge loan. When his friend defaulted on the loan, the husband had some of his salary taken from him by the lender. Her family had to face a devastating situation. Having a six-member family, they were spiraling into greater debt each month. She began to feel that she could no longer depend on her husband's income and decided to find a job. She fasted and prayed to God to show her the way. One day, as she was praying all night in church, a brilliant light shone upon her. She saw a vision in the light. She saw a small building with a shop on the first floor and a place of residence on the second. She was instantly convinced it was God's answer to her prayer. In the morning, she returned home with joy and conviction. Before the month was over, she did find a small store where she was able to start a small business and helped support her family. Finally, they got out of debt.

In much the same way, the first step to a productive life is to let light shine into your life. Before light shines upon you and shows you the path, do not act according to your own way. The reasons many people today are trapped with no way out is because they depend on and follow their own ways and means.

If you truly want to live in success and blessing, no matter how much darkness may seem to surround you, you must wait and pray for the guiding light of God. When it shines down upon you, you will see exactly what you must do.

Such light may come to you as a revelation, a dream or a vision. It may come as you are reading the Bible. There are other ways light might come to you. When Christians fail to wait for such guiding light of the Holy Spirit and run ahead of Him, it always leads to failure. You must kneel down and pray, and then wait. You must firmly command yourself saying,

"Light shall come upon me. Let there be light in my life."

chapter 13

Look Up to Heaven, and Believe in Miracles

"And God said, 'Let there be an expanse between the waters to separate water from water.' So God made the expanse and separated the water under the expanse from the water above it. And it was so. God called the expanse 'sky.' And there was evening, and there was morning the second day" (Genesis 1:6-8).

On the second day God said, "Let there be an expanse between the waters to separate water from water." Then the waters, which had filled the world, were separated into the upper and the lower water. The sky appeared between them.

Although you have received the guiding light in your life through the first step, your life may still be full of the waters of despair. In the second step, the waters of despair must be separated, and the sky of hope must appear in your life. That means that God stays with us and performs great miracles through His Word.

Just as when the world was being created, "the sky" must appear in our lives. Then the gate of Heaven in the sky, beyond human ways and means, will open and we will hear the voice of faith from Heaven, "'If you can'? Everything is possible for him who believes"

Is the sky of hope in your life? Just as the sky above us extends endlessly, does the sky of hope spread in your life? Then call out loudly, "O Father, I do believe there will be a miracle in my life!"

You must believe that God's miracles will take place in your business. You must believe that they will take place in your home. You must expect such miracles as you pray.

Those who do not have the sky of hope opened up in their lives cannot experience the miracle of Heaven. It is because they do not regard the Word of God as powerful. To those who do not expect miracles, miracles never happen.

There is nothing more miserable and meaningless than faith without hope. While Noah stayed in the ark, he never saw the flood. In the ark, there were three decks and a door on the side. Once all the animals and his family entered the ark, God closed the door. They could only look out through one single window on the ceiling. What they could see through the window was the sky.

Rain fell on the earth for forty days and forty nights. The earth was flooded by the waters for 150 days. Noah was surrounded by such a miserable environment, but he looked up only at the sky.

What does this signify? No matter how much turbulence and hardship there may be in your life, you should look up to the sky and believe in the promises of God and His miracles.

The Bible is the window that can help us look at the sky. Without the Bible, there is no way to look up at the sky. Through the Word of God we are comforted, and we receive faith, courage, and boldness to keep our eyes on the sky.

Therefore, you must not be lazy in hearing and reading the Word of God. You must always have faith that expects miracles. You must have faith, expecting tomorrow will be better than today, and next year will be better than this year. Such people with the wide-open gate of Heaven cannot help but succeed. Those who look to the waters of despair will drown in the deep pit of despair. Those who look at the sky of hope will ride upon the silver wings of success as they fly through the sky.

chapter 14

Make a Definite Plan

"And God said, 'Let the water under the sky be gathered to one place, and let dry ground appear,' And it was so. God called the dry ground 'land,' and the gathered waters he called 'seas.' And God saw that it was good Then God said, 'Let the land produce vegetation: seed-bearing plants and trees on the land that bear fruit with seed in it, according to their various finds.' And it was so" (Genesis 1:9-11).

When the land was underwater, there was nothing. However, when dry ground appeared above the water through God's command, it began to produce various vegetation, plants and trees. What does the land symbolize in our lives? It is similar to making a definite plan, setting a goal and a time limit, according to the revelation of God.

God does not bless vague plans. If you have the vision and desire to revive your church, you must set a definite goal. And in order to achieve the goal, you must have a detailed plan on how many new converts you will bring to church every week.

If you have a desire to start a business, you must begin making plans, as you trust in the miracles of God. You must decide what kind of business you want to be in and make detailed plans including the scope and size, the contacts, daily sales projection, profit margin and so on. This represents "the land" in your life.

Upon such land, when you pray to God for miracles, He will indeed answer you. When God does so, your life will bear the fruit of miracles and blessings in abundance. No matter how solid the land may be under water, if it does not rise above, it cannot be shown on the map. Land not shown on the map is not really "land."

Just as the land appeared above the water, a definite plan and vision must appear in your heart. Then upon that land, God will bless you so that you may yield great fruit. However, God will never bless a vague plan, even though you try to make it succeed. It will never come to fruition.

chapter 15

Let the Sun, the Moon, and the Stars Shine Brightly

"And God said, 'Let there be lights in the expanse of the sky to separate the day from the night, and let them serve as signs to mark seasons and days and years, and let them be lights in the expanse of the sky to give light on the earth.' And it was so. God made two great lights— the greater light to govern the day and the lesser light to govern the night. He also made the stars. God set them in the expanse of the sky to give light on the earth"
(Genesis 1:14-17).

On the fourth day of creation, God made the sun, the moon and the stars. Did you know that God also created the sun, the moon and the stars inside your mind?

Our wisdom is the sun, and emotion is the moon in our minds. The intelligence that helps us out of a difficult bind are the stars.

Why did God give us these things? It is because once we have made a concrete plan, God desires us to use our wisdom, emotion and intelligence to carry out the plan.

If a man goes out to a field in cold winter and prays, "God, bless me with a great crop," and sows seeds upon that field, he is not sane. He must plant seeds in spring to harvest in fall. In a similar way, just because we know God's will, it does not mean we can simply carry out His will anytime and anywhere. Using our wisdom, emotion, and intelligence, we must distinguish God's times and signs.

Sometimes our minds may be covered with clouds of anger and greed. We must not allow anger and greed in our hearts.

Osaka Medical College published this report, "A dog which had been completely bound for four hours, then brought to a wild fury by beating, was found to contain a surprising amount of 'cyanogen,' a poisonous chemical in its brain. The amount was enough to kill 80 sheep."

It is the same way with a person. When you become extremely angry, a poisonous matter is produced in your body, and it causes physiological change and affects all organs of your body.

No matter what you do, do not be overly greedy nor easily brought to anger. If you avoid the above two, the sun, the moon and the stars will shine brightly in your mind. Then, whatever you do, you will be able to succeed.

chapter 16

Have the Mind of Wealth

"And God said, 'Let the water teem with living creatures, and let birds fly above the earth across the expanse of the sky.' So God created the great creatures of the sea and every living and moving thing with which the water teems, according to their kinds, and every winged bird according to its kind ... God made the wild animals according to their kinds, the livestock according to their kinds, and all the creatures that move along the ground according to their kinds. And God saw that it was good" (Genesis 1:20-25).

On the fifth and sixth day of creation, God filled the land, the sky, and the sea with living creatures. In the sky there are birds, on land there are wild animals, and in the sea there are many fish.

Just imagine you are the master of such a world. What do you feel? Do you feel you are poor? Probably not. You are probably feeling, "I am very wealthy."

You must have the mind of wealth. Let the birds fly, the animals play, and the fish swim in your heart. You must fill yourself with thoughts of great wealth.

If you send out brain waves that you are greatly wealthy, it brings wealth. Thinking about success brings success, and thinking about blessing brings blessing. Then your life and circumstances will be filled with success and blessing.

Although you desire to be rich and wealthy, if you continually think or say, "I can't. Not me. I can't succeed in the life of faith. I am poor. How can I live on this poor pay?" You can never get out of failure and poverty if you think this way. Only the negative things, like poverty, destitution, and illness, will gather around you.

As such, if you desire to live a successful life of wealth, you must always have a picture of yourself as a wealthy person. You must imagine your heart is like the land, the sky, and the sea filled with all kinds of living creatures. You must think it consciously. So let the mind of wealth always take its place in your heart.

In the parable of the talent (Matthew 25:14-30), the servant who had received five talents and gained five more was given the ten talents and also one more as a gift. On the other hand, the servant who had received one talent and buried it in the ground, grumbling at his master, was deprived of even that one talent.

> *"For everyone who has will be given more, and he will have an abundance. Whoever does not have, even what he has will be taken from him" (Matthew 25:20).*

Concerning your business and your health, at all times you must have the mind of wealth. When you do so, God will add to your wealth and make your life abundant. I bless you and pray that through the mind of wealth you should be given more, and enjoy abundance all the time, everywhere, and in everything.

chapter 17

Be an Absolute Optimist

"God blessed them and said to them, 'Be fruitful and increase in number; fill the earth and subdue it. Rule over the fish of the sea and the birds of the air and over every living creature that moves on the ground" (Genesis 1:28).

The sixth step to a successful and productive life is to live as those who are created in God's image to enjoy His blessings, subduing and ruling over all things on the earth.

We must remember that we were created in the image and likeness of God. Although humankind had lost that image of God due to the fall of Adam and Eve, through the blood of Jesus Christ, we have restored that lost image. We can now stand before God proudly as we worship and praise Him.

We must also realize that we are nothing more than the "image and likeness" of God. If we forget our places and try to reach up to the place of God, we will find great destruction, just as the Tower of Babel had fallen. We must always acknowledge God's authority over all things, obey Him in humility, and live our lives centering on Him.

God commanded humankind to subdue the earth. Such work cannot be done while sitting idle. Such work requires the attitude to devote all one's might. You eat when others eat, and you sleep when others sleep. If you do so and pray to be more blessed than others and to live a successful life, it is very wrong.

In order to be a ruler, you must be responsible. A person without a sense of responsibility is unqualified to be a ruler.

A person who feels no responsibility for his family does not have the right to be called the head of that household. God answers those who are responsible. To them God gives the right and power to rule.

For us to conquer and subdue this world, we must have positive minds. Those who think and say negative words cannot conquer anything. However, those who have positive minds always say: "I am a child of God. I am a conqueror over my circumstances. I subdue all illnesses in the name of Jesus Christ. As Christ was wounded, I have been healed. I subdue my imperfect personality and rule over it. I have been created in the image of God and in the name of Christ, I can change flaws in my character."

If you have such a positive attitude, conquering every environment and ruling over it, God will give you greater wealth and happiness.

chapter 18

Pray Until You Are at Peace

*"Thus the heavens and the earth were
completed in all their vast array. By the
seventh day God had finished the work he
had been doing; so on the seventh day he
rested from all his work" (Genesis 2:1, 2).*

After having created the heavens and the earth
and all things in them, God rested. Rest is also
necessary in our lives. The last step to a productive
life is peace of mind and rest.

There was a young man with a very hopeful and bright future. He decided to write down all that he hoped to accomplish in his life. He wrote, "Fame, wealth, health, a beautiful wife, bright children, authority …"

He filled a notebook with these things. He took that notebook to an old professor whom he had always admired.

"Professor, I've written down all that is important to me and what I hope to achieve. I will absolutely succeed in acquiring them."

The professor read through the notebook, then smiled as he said, "There is something of utmost importance, which you have left out."

"What is that?" the young man asked.

The professor wrote at the bottom of the list, "Peace of mind."

That is right. We may obtain fame and wealth, but if we do not have peace of mind, we cannot truly experience happiness and joy. Peace of mind is the most important thing in this world. This is the reason why God rested on the last day of creation. The beginning and end of all work belongs to God. It was God who started to create the world and completed it. There is nothing created by humanity in the world. Adam did not have to do anything on his first day because God created him after having completed the creation of the world. Creating and operating the universe is God's work, while people believe, worship, and praise Him.

Adam and Eve, however, were tricked by Satan, and they tried to make their own world and to work by themselves. It led to their fall, and they were driven out.

Work is a special right of God, and belongs to Him. Therefore, we must turn over all work to Him in order to live successful lives.

Do you have problems? Turn them over to the Lord. Come before God, and call out to Him and let Him take them. When you do so, you will indeed feel peace of mind. It is a sign that God is carrying that burden for you.

> *"Come to me, all you who are weary and*
> *burdened, and I will give you rest. Take*
> *my yoke upon you and learn from me, for*
> *I am gentle and humble in heart, and you*
> *will find rest for your souls. For my yoke is*
> *easy and my burden is light"*
> *(Matthew 11:28-30).*

Whatever you do, you must first kneel down before God and pray until you feel peace of mind wash over you, and then begin the work. If you begin any work without peace of mind, you must take responsibility for the work. However, if you start the work after you receive peace of mind, God who is the Alpha and the Omega will take the responsibility for the work and accomplish it.

DR. DAVID YONGGI CHO is the founder and senior pastor of Yoido Full Gospel Church in Seoul, Korea, which has more than 750,000 members. World renowned as a powerful speaker, Dr. Cho is the author of many books including *The Fourth Dimension*, *Solving Life's Problems*, *The Holy Spirit—My Senior Partner* and *Spiritual Leadership for the New Millennium*.